GANGSTER HAMSTERS

By Anthony Smith

 Published by Markosia Enterprises, PO BOX 3477, Barnet, Hertfordshire, EN5 9HN. FIRST PRINTING, October 2016. Harry Markos, Director.

ISBN 978-1-909276-96-3

www.markosia.com

FOR **MARKOSIA ENTERPRISES** LTD

HARRY MARKOS
PUBLISHER AND
MANAGING PARTNER

ANDY BRIGGS
CREATIVE
CONSULTANT

GM JORDAN
SPECIAL PROJECTS
CO-ORDINATOR

MEIRION JONES
MARKETING
DIRECTOR

ANNIKA EADE
MEDIA MANAGER

IAN SHARMAN
EDITOR IN CHIEF

Floyd
Rocco
Mooky

DEPARTURES
NOTHING TO DECLARE

Sleeping with the goldfish

"Don't ever be a rat."

"Made it, Ma! ... Top of the wheel!"

"What do you mean furry? ... Furry how? ...
How am I furry?"

Bug deal

"Look out! ... It's a wise guy!"

"Relax, you're just going for a little ride."

"We're under surveillance again, boys."

Gangster's mole

"You dirty rat!"

Menu
Sunflower seeds - 50c
Pumpkin seeds - 50c
Mixed seeds - 50c
Cold DRINKS here!

Seedy joint

"Hey, buddy... you looking for a little extra protection?"

St. Valentine's Day Mouseacre

“You really are a nutcase, you know that?”

Squeakeasy

“I wish I wuz big just once!”

Gumshoe detective

When gangsters took over the Big Apple

"They're good fellers!"

"Looks like somebody wacked him."

"Yeah, that's right, we're talking to you... ***you pussy!***"

“You got a big mouth, pal!”

"He's a made man."

"You're going down, you sucker!"

"Get your paws off me!"

Ferret Bureau of Investigation

"Go climb up your thumb!"

"Looks like we're eating Al Fresco."

"He said 'we're in on a big deal'... no, waitaminute... ***'wheel'!"***

"He's taken care of... we made it look like roadkill."

"Remind me... who's bright idea was it to take a trip back to the 'old country'?"

"He's squirreled his stash away in here!"

Roadkill funeral

The Hole in the Wall Gang

"***Ahhh!*** ... I've been bugged!"

“I say we rub him out!”

Mickey Fin

“He’s a cold-blooded killer!”

Angoras with dirty faces

"Try to weasel your way out of this one!"

"How did I ever get into this racket?"

"We're just busting your balls!"

Bootlegging

"Stay on this mutt's tail!"

China Town

"Slug him again!"

Polecat dancing club

"You talk too much!"

"As far back as I can remember, I always wanted to be an accountant."

"You squeakin' at me?"

"I'm starting to think he doesn't mind this!"

Stool pigeon

The Cosy Nostra

"Your partner's in luck... we're outta concrete!"

Matches Maloney

Guinea pigs on patrol

“He’s got a wire on him!”

"Whaddya mean, I don't take you out anywhere? ...
You say you don't like it above ground!"

"That's ***guinea*** pig to you, chum!"

"You wanna see your guy again, give us plenty of the folding green stuff Yeah that's right *cabbage!*"

*"Didn't I tell you not to get anything big?! ...
Didn't I tell you not to attract attention?!"*

"He just croaked!"

"I'm starting to think one of us is a rat!"

"You lyin' low too, huh?"

Failed getaway

Spending time in the can

Tomcat gun

“Don’t touch me, you worm sucker!”

“They’ve made us a banofee we can’t refuse!”

“Just when I thought I was out, they pull me back in!”

“That’s it... I’m going straight!”

The Big Sleep

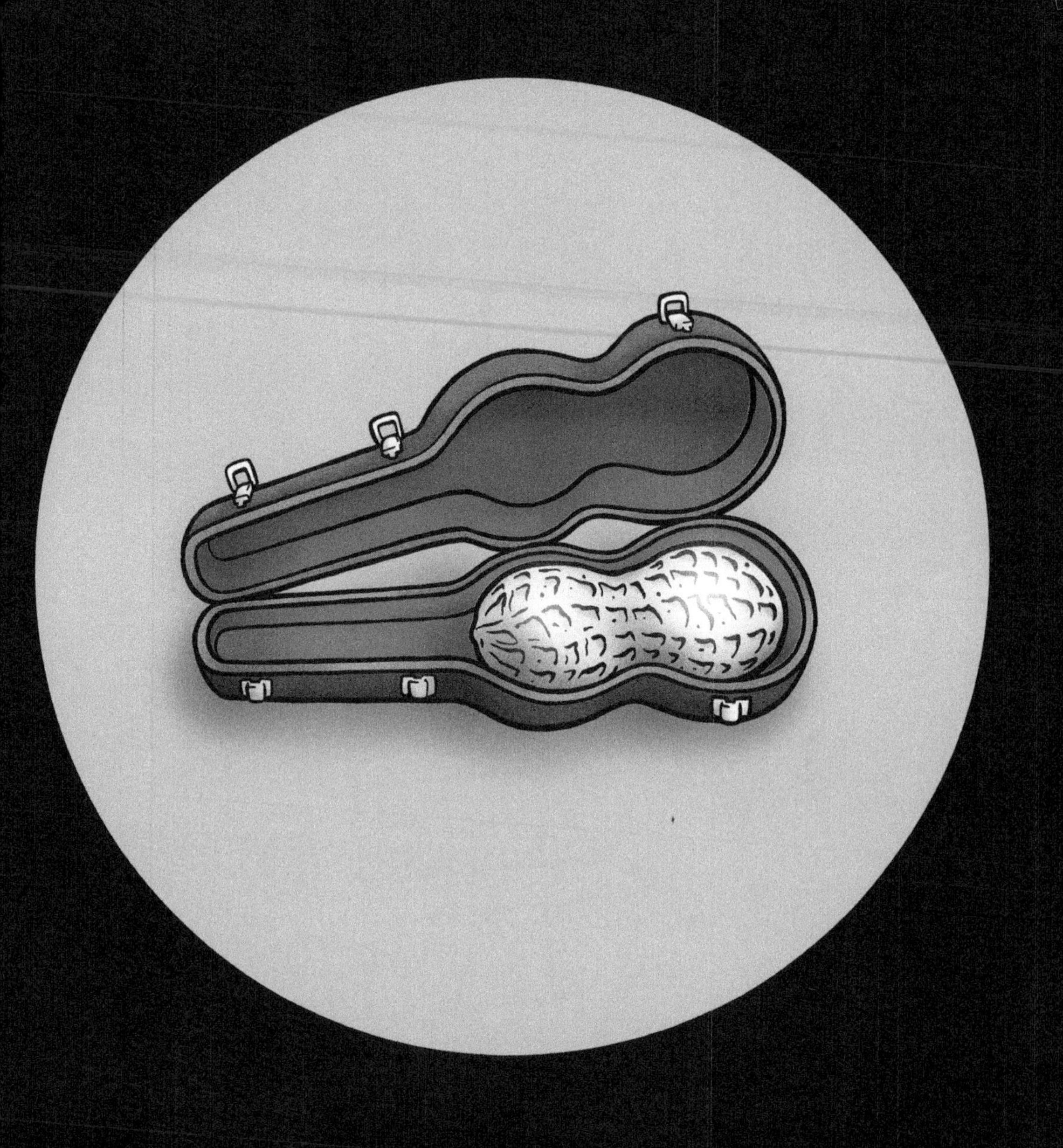

Mug shots
FERRET BUREAU OF INVESTIGATION
Paw prints

Wise guys
The crows
FBI Headquarters
The bats
Mickey Finn
Good fellers
The Big Apple
Pussy
The squirrels
Matches Maloney
Made man
China Town
Gangster Hamsters
Guinea Pig Cops
Angora rabbits
The can
Jail Guard Shrews
Poker Club
Hole in the Wall Gang
The parrot
The mutt
Gangster's moles
The rats
Squeakeasys
Polecat dancing club
Snooker hall
Seedy joint
FBI
Floyd
Rocco
Mooky
Known Gangster Hamsters

RAT-
A-TAT

Anthony Smith began his career at Marvel UK, working as a cartoonist on their line of children's comics. From there he went on to work for several other publishers on a variety of more mature titles.

He then took a detour into advertising where he worked as a writer and art director for a few top agencies in London, creating campaigns for various brands.

In recent years he has contributed a daily cartoon feature to the Metro newspaper and various random cartoons to Private Eye magazine, as well as working on his new venture, Gangster Hamsters for Markosia.

Special thanks to John Donnelly, Karen Bates and Irene Hoffman.

MARKOSIA

LEADING THE WAY

Lightning Source UK Ltd.
Milton Keynes UK
UKOW07f1949031016

284026UK00018B/17/P

9 781909 276963